KU-236-810

South Dublin Libraries

www.southdublinlibraries.ie

YOUR PASSPORT TO
ARGENTINA

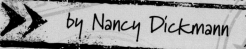

by Nancy Dickmann

raintree
a Capstone company — publishers for children

Raintree is an imprint of Capstone Global Library Limited, a company incorporated in
England and Wales having its registered office at 264 Banbury Road, Oxford, OX2 7DY –
Registered company number: 6695582

www.raintree.co.uk
myorders@raintree.co.uk

Text © Capstone Global Library Limited 2022
The moral rights of the proprietor have been asserted.

All rights reserved. No part of this publication may be reproduced in any form or by any
means (including photocopying or storing it in any medium by electronic means and
whether or not transiently or incidentally to some other use of this publication) without
the written permission of the copyright owner, except in accordance with the provisions of
the Copyright, Designs and Patents Act 1988 or under the terms of a licence issued by the
Copyright Licensing Agency, 5th Floor, Shackleton House, 4 Battle Bridge Lane, London
SE1 2HX (www.cla.co.uk). Applications for the copyright owner's written permission
should be addressed to the publisher.

Edited by Clare Lewis
Designed by Juliette Peters
Original illustrations © Capstone Global Library Limited 2022
Picture research by Tracy Cummins
Production by Laura Manthe
Originated by Capstone Global Library Ltd
Printed and bound in India

978 1 3982 1506 1 (hardback)
978 1 3982 1505 4 (paperback)

British Library Cataloguing in Publication Data
A full catalogue record for this book is available from the British Library.

Acknowledgements
We would like to thank the following for permission to reproduce photographs: Capstone:
Eric Gohl, 5; Getty Images: AFP PHOTO/JUAN MABROMATA, 24, Bettmann, 11;
Shutterstock: Analia Valeria Urani, 21, Bisual Photo, 27, buenaventura, 25, Diego Grandi,
6, emilyz21, 14, Jose Breton- Pics Action, 26, Kobby Dagan, 29, Mariano Gaspar, 23, Ondrej
Prosicky, 16, R.M. Nunes, 13, saiko3p, 9, sunsinger, 19, ThiagoSantos, Cover. Design
elements: iStockphoto: Yevhenii Dubinko; Shutterstock: Julinzy, MicroOne, octopusaga,
pingebat.

Every effort has been made to contact copyright holders of material reproduced in this
book. Any omissions will be rectified in subsequent printings if notice is given to the
publisher.

All the internet addresses (URLs) given in this book were valid at the time of going to
press. However, due to the dynamic nature of the internet, some addresses may have
changed, or sites may have changed or ceased to exist since publication. While the author
and publisher regret any inconvenience this may cause readers, no responsibility for any
such changes can be accepted by either the author or the publisher.

CONTENTS

Words in **bold** are in the glossary.

CHAPTER ONE

WELCOME TO ARGENTINA!

A giant river of ice tumbles down a slope into a deep lake. Behind it, mountains reach towards the sky. Opposite, a river descends for hundreds of kilometres and ends in the blue waters of the ocean. The ice river is the Perito Moreno Glacier in Argentina. It is one of the country's many natural wonders. It is in a remote location. But it still draws thousands of visitors each year.

Argentina is a large country in South America. More than 45 million people live there. Most of them speak Spanish. This is because Spanish explorers settled in the area hundreds of years ago. Since then, people have come from many other countries. There are also many **indigenous** people. Their ancestors lived there long before the Spanish arrived.

MAP OF ARGENTINA

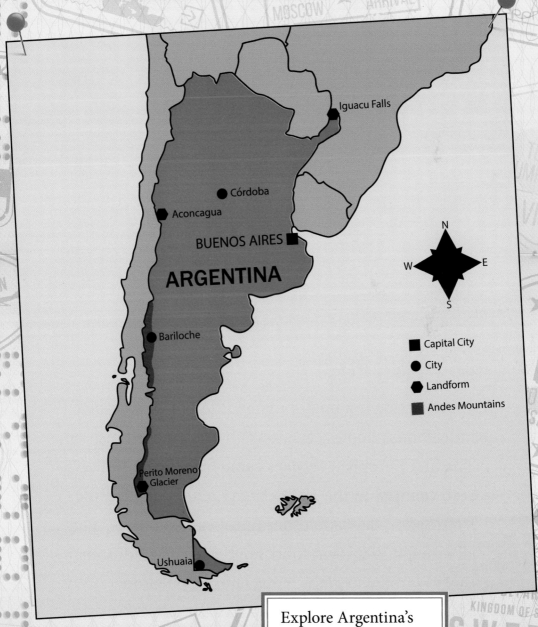

Iguacu Falls

Córdoba

Aconcagua

BUENOS AIRES

ARGENTINA

Bariloche

Perito Moreno Glacier

Ushuaia

N
W   E
S

■ Capital City

● City

⬡ Landform

■ Andes Mountains

Explore Argentina's cities and landmarks.

Many of Argentina's cities have a European feel.

MELTING POT

Argentina is a mix of many different cultures. Its indigenous peoples each have their own customs. The first European **settlers** came from Spain in the 16th century. In the 1800s, many more people came from Spain, Italy and other European countries. They all brought their own food, language and traditions. By 1914, many regions had a large population of Europeans.

FACT FILE

OFFICIAL NAME: .... ARGENTINE REPUBLIC
POPULATION: 45,164,434
LAND AREA: .... 2,736,690 SQ KM (1,056,642 SQ. MI.)
CAPITAL: .... BUENOS AIRES
MONEY: .... ARGENTINE PESO
GOVERNMENT: .... PRESIDENTIAL REPUBLIC
LANGUAGE: .... SPANISH
GEOGRAPHY: Argentina forms most of the southern part of South America. It has a long western border with Chile. Its northern end borders Bolivia, Paraguay, Brazil and Uruguay. To the east is the Atlantic Ocean.
NATURAL RESOURCES: Argentina has lead, zinc, tin, copper, oil and plenty of land for growing crops and raising cattle.

CITY AND COUNTRYSIDE

Argentina has beautiful cities. They include Buenos Aires and Córdoba. There are also vast plains and rainforests. There are high mountains too. The tallest is Aconcagua. It is the highest peak in South America. Argentina extends a long way south. Its tip is only 1,238 kilometres (769 miles) north of Antarctica.

CHAPTER TWO

HISTORY OF ARGENTINA

Long ago, Argentina was made up of small tribes. Most of them hunted for food. They gathered plants to eat. Some groups grew crops and raised llamas. They also built small cities of stone. Some areas of northwest Argentina were part of the mighty **Inca Empire**.

INVADERS

Everything changed when Spanish explorers arrived. They explored the coast in the early 1500s. Then they moved slowly inland. Spanish settlers built towns, including Buenos Aires. They raised cattle and grew crops such as corn and potatoes.

Spanish settlers often treated the indigenous people badly. Unlike the indigenous people, the Spanish had horses and guns. They used them to control the people. They forced many to become Catholics. The settlers also often enslaved people and forced them to work. Many indigenous people were killed or died of diseases brought by the Spanish.

Spanish settlers built many churches in Argentina.

FACT

Argentina's name comes from a Latin word meaning silver. Early explorers hoped to find gold and silver there. They believed stories about a mountain range made entirely of silver.

TIMELINE OF ARGENTINIAN HISTORY

PRE-1400: Many indigenous tribes with very different cultures live on the land we now call Argentina.

LATE 1400S: The Inca Empire conquers land in northwest Argentina.

1516: The Spanish explorer Juan Díaz de Solís sails up the Río de la Plata.

1536: Pedro de Mendoza founds the city of Buenos Aires.

1613: Argentina's first university is founded in Córdoba.

1776: Spain sets up the vice royalty of the Río de la Plata, which includes modern Argentina, Uruguay and Paraguay, as well as part of Bolivia. The capital is Buenos Aires.

1806-1807: British troops attack Argentina but are forced to retreat.

1810: With the Spanish king overthrown, local landowners set up a government.

1816: Argentina declares its independence from Spain.

1826: Bernardino Rivadavia becomes the first president of Argentina.

1865-1870: Argentina, Brazil and Uruguay defeat Paraguay in war.

1945: Argentina enters World War II on the side of the **Allies**.

1946: Juan Perón is elected president.

1982: British troops defeat Argentina's attempt to take control of the Falkland Islands.

INDEPENDENCE

Spain continued to rule Argentina until 1808. Then, in Europe, France imprisoned and replaced the Spanish king. People in Argentina now had no king. Could they rule themselves? Local officials took control. They set up a government in 1810. Later, in 1816, they declared that Argentina was **independent**.

BECOMING A MODERN NATION

After independence, the country still wasn't united. There was fighting for several years. By 1853, the country finally agreed on a **constitution**. Many Argentines also continued to fight the indigenous people until the late 1800s. They took almost all of the indigenous people's land to use for farming. In the late 1800s, Argentina's economy boomed. Immigrants from Europe poured in.

THE 20TH CENTURY

Juan Perón became president in 1946. He gave new rights to workers. He improved their pay. Perón and his wife, Eva, did a lot to help the poor, and they were very popular. But Perón was harsh to his enemies. Eva died in 1952 and Perón was forced out in 1955. He returned to power in 1973.

Eva Perón is still remembered as an important figure in Argentina.

CHAPTER THREE

AREAS TO EXPLORE

Argentina is a popular country to explore. Almost 6 million people visit each year. They come for the country's natural beauty. They visit historic cities. Many people start their tour to Antarctica in Argentina.

FANTASTIC FALLS

The Paraná is Argentina's longest river. It merges with other rivers before flowing into the Atlantic Ocean. The Iguaçu River is one of these. Just before it joins, it plunges over a cliff. This creates a series of stunning waterfalls. The falls are horseshoe-shaped. They are three times as wide as Niagara Falls! Some of the falls are 82 metres (269 feet) high.

The Iguaçu Falls lie on the border between Argentina and Brazil.

FACT

Fossils of a giant dinosaur called *Argentinosaurus* have been found in Argentina. It is the biggest land dinosaur ever discovered.

Aconcagua is 6,959 m (22,831 feet) high.

MIGHTY MOUNTAINS

The Andes run along Argentina's western edge. This mountain range has tall, jagged peaks. Some of them are **volcanoes**. Many are covered in snow all year round. Tourists love to explore the mountains. But only serious climbers tackle Aconcagua!

Many animals make their home in the Andes. Vicuna are related to llamas. They graze on the slopes of the mountains. Another relative, the guanaco, lives here too. High above, condors soar through the air. These large birds scan the ground for dead animals to eat.

PATAGONIA

Many people come to Patagonia, a region in the south. This area is high and windy. The air is dry. There are lakes, mountains and **glaciers**. On the coast, visitors can see whales, seals and penguins.

GLACIERS

Glaciers flow down some of the mountains. They are like rivers of ice. Some flow into lakes. There is a wall of ice where they meet the water. Huge icebergs break off and float away.

The bush dog is rare and was once believed to be extinct.

THE PAMPAS

Further north, there is a vast **grassland**. It is called
the Pampas. Farmers grow soya beans, grapes and
grains. Ranchers raise cattle and sheep. There are also
wild animals such as foxes and bush dogs. Viscachas
live here too. These rodents look like a cross between
a rabbit and a squirrel.

EXCITING CITIES

Many visitors come to the capital, Buenos Aires. It is on the banks of the wide Río de la Plata. More than 15 million people live there. Many of the buildings look European. There are restaurants, plazas and shops. Buenos Aires is divided into neighbourhoods. Each one has its own character.

Córdoba is in the centre of the country. The Pampas lies to the south. Córdoba has many historic buildings. They were built by the Spanish settlers. Tourists often visit ranches in the surrounding area.

FACT

Of all the cities in the world, Ushuaia is the furthest south. Here, tourists board ships to Antarctica. The trip takes about 48 hours.

CHAPTER FOUR

DAILY LIFE

Life in Argentina's cities is similar to life in Spain or Italy. Shops in some areas close for a long lunch break, then reopen in the afternoon. In the hot summer, it's a good time for a nap! Shops stay open into the evening. People enjoy meeting up at cafes and restaurants. There are museums, shops and art galleries. Fewer people live in the countryside. Many of them work as farmers and ranchers.

TIME FOR SCHOOL

Children go to school from Monday to Friday. In many schools, there is a morning session and an afternoon session. Most students only attend one. They have the rest of the day to complete homework, play sports and practise hobbies.

A small number of people in the Pampas still follow the gaucho lifestyle.

GAUCHOS

The gaucho is an important part of Argentina's culture. In the past, these cowboys rode across the Pampas. They tended cattle, and slept in small mud huts. Gauchos were independent and self-reliant. People in Argentina love reading stories and singing songs about gauchos.

FOOD AND DRINK

People in Argentina love to share meals with friends and family. The food is a mix of cultures. There are many Spanish and Italian dishes. There are also foods and drinks from the indigenous tribes. These include maté, a type of tea.

POPULAR FOODS

Argentina is famous for beef. At an asado, people grill beef and other meat to share. People also make empanadas. These pastry pockets are filled with meat and cheese and served hot. There are many different fillings.

People in Argentina love sweet foods too. Dulce de leche is a type of caramel made by heating sweetened milk. It is spread on pancakes and toast. It is also used as an ingredient in other dishes, such as biscuits called *alfajores*.

Argentines eat more beef than people in most other countries.

CHIMICHURRI

Argentines love putting this sauce on grilled meat. They also use it to add flavour to other dishes. Many families have their own version of the recipe.

Ingredients:
- 30 grams fresh parsley
- 12 grams fresh oregano
- 2 spring onions
- 4 cloves of garlic
- 180 ml apple cider vinegar
- juice of 1 lemon
- 240 ml olive oil
- salt and pepper
- pinch of crushed chili flakes (optional)

Instructions:
1. Remove the stems from the parsley and oregano, then chop the leaves.
2. Ask an adult to finely chop the spring onions and garlic.
3. Put all the ingredients into a bowl and let it sit for at least half an hour before eating.

CHAPTER FIVE

HOLIDAYS AND CELEBRATIONS

About 80 per cent of people in Argentina are Catholic. However, most of them don't go to church often. Even so, Catholic holidays are very important to them. On Christmas Eve, some families go to church. After that, they have dinner and a party. Fireworks shoot into the sky.

6 January is Three Kings Day. The night before, children put shoes outside their door or window. They also leave grass for the Kings' camels. When they wake up, the shoes are filled with gifts.

FACT

Argentina is in the southern hemisphere. Seasons there are the opposite of seasons in the UK. This means that in Argentina, Christmas is in the summer!

Before the start of Lent, Argentines celebrate **Carnival** with parades and street parties.

OTHER RELIGIONS

Some people in Argentina are Muslim or Jewish. They celebrate holidays in their own religion. These include Ramadan and Eid al-Fitr for Muslims. Jewish people celebrate holidays such as Hanukkah and Rosh Hashanah.

NATIONAL DAY

Argentines celebrate the Anniversary of the First National Government on 25 May. They remember the people who fought for their country's freedom. Politicians give speeches. There are marches and concerts. Churches have special services, and theatres put on plays.

Families celebrate together by making special meals. These often include a hearty stew called *locro*. It is made of beans, squash and corn. It usually has meat too. There might be potatoes or yams.

People gather for the 25 May celebrations.

Bariloche's beautiful location makes it popular with skiers and hikers.

SNOW FESTIVAL

The city of Bariloche is at the foot of the Andes. It is famous as a centre for skiing. At the end of July, the city hosts a big celebration. This marks the start of the skiing season. At dusk, a parade of skiers carries torches down the mountain. There are fireworks, races and games.

CHAPTER SIX

SPORT AND RECREATION

Football is the most popular sport in Argentina. People play on **amateur** teams and go to professional matches. Diego Maradona and Lionel Messi are both from Argentina. Many people think they are two of the best footballers ever.

Argentina's national team has won the World Cup twice. They have been runners-up three times. Their main rival is another South American country, Brazil.

Lionel Messi became captain of Argentina's football team in 2011.

Padel is played with plastic rackets.

OTHER SPORTS

Rugby union is also popular in Argentina. There are many amateur teams. The best players often go to play for clubs in Europe. People in Argentina also love basketball. Millions of people play a type of tennis called *padel*. The court is small, with walls around it. Players can hit the ball off the walls.

RIDING SPORTS

Argentina is famous for polo. This sport is played on horseback. Riders use a long mallet to hit the ball. They try to get it into the goal. There is a similar sport called *pato*. It is hundreds of years old. Riders try to throw a ball into a goal.

EL GALLITO CIEGO

The name of this game is Spanish for "Little Blind Rooster". It can be played by a group of children. All you need is a blindfold and enough space to run around.

1. Choose one person to be the rooster and blindfold them.
2. Turn the rooster around a few times.
3. Everyone runs, and the rooster has to try to catch them.
4. When someone is caught, the rooster has to guess who they are. If they guess wrong, they have to catch someone else. If they guess right, the person they caught becomes the rooster.

Tango dancers show lots of emotion in their performance.

TANGO

Tango is a slow, dramatic dance. It is also a style of music. Tango started in Buenos Aires in the late 1800s. It is a mix of African, European and local styles. Visitors can watch dancers perform in theatres and at cafes and clubs. Today, ballroom dancers around the world perform the tango.

GLOSSARY

Allies
countries that fought with Britain and the United States in World Wars I and II

amateur
person who does something for fun rather than as a job

Carnival
celebration that happens immediately before the period of prayer and fasting known as Lent

constitution
document that outlines a country's basic laws and how its government is set up

glacier
large body of ice that moves slowly down a slope

grassland
large area of land with grasses but few trees

Inca Empire
empire ruled by a group called the Incas, who lived in the Andes Mountains in the 1400s and early 1500s

independent
not ruled over by anyone else

indigenous
native to a place

settlers
people who come to a new area to set up farms and towns

volcano
mountain with a crater at the top, through which lava, gas and ash can erupt

FIND OUT MORE

BOOKS

Geography Matters in the Inca Empire
(Geography Matters in Ancient Civilizations),
Melanie Waldron (Raintree, 2015)

Introducing South America (Introducing Continents),
Anita Ganeri (Raintree, 2013)

Our World in Pictures: Countries, Cultures, People and Places: A Visual Encyclopedia of the World, DK
(DK Children, 2020)

WEBSITES

www.bbc.co.uk/bitesize/topics/z849q6f
Explore the natural world, including mountains and volcanoes.

www.dkfindout.com/uk/history/incas/inca-empire
Find out more about the Inca Empire.

INDEX

OTHER BOOKS IN THIS SERIES